THEM

poems 1999–2002
by Omar Shapli

Published by:

Baltimore, Maryland

www.twentythreebooks.com

Acknowledgements

"Global Positioning" first appeared in the *New Orleans Review*, Volume 29, #1, June 2003.

"Overheard by Tillinghast in a Boston Bar" first appeared in *Main Street Rag*, Volume 10, #3, Fall 2005.

for Tryntje

and the crows

Contents

To Begin With…

Seeing can be a difficult, an arduous operation.

We lived a number of years in a 9th floor apartment overlooking
Houston Street, on the fraying fringe of Greenwich Village. We did
plenty of persisting and the kids a lot of growing up in that place,
and through the picture-window they and we watched with lurid
fascination the floor-by-floor ascent of a tiny derrick perched like
a nesting falcon on the steel-and-concrete armature which finally
became the second of the tradecenter towers. Completed, those
gleaming megaliths dominated our view of lower Manhattan. It
would perhaps be an exaggeration to say we developed affection for
them, but they were markers: they among much else defined our
world.

Then came a morning decades later and worlds away from that
place. My wife had called me to the TV, and there we were, facing
a view eerily identical in angle and perspective to the one that had
greeted— or mocked or awed or irritated—us every morning, back
in the days.

For us it sparked a sudden and a wrenching restaging: openmouthed
children, fingers and noses pressed against the glass, seeing *as
it happened* the absolutely ungraspable slaughter of thousands of
bewildered human creatures, just a stroll down Lower Broadway and
a few blocks off to the west. The children were *our* children… and
were us.

Attempts are made to contain such things. We are exhorted to stand
firm, close ranks, stay the course. We are told what *they* are, what *we*
are, how to name what is happening, and perhaps that is as it should
be. Indeed, the categorizing of events and people is a well-established
method of saving us from seeing them. Without that category-word
Enemy, war would be, if not impossible, far less sparing of our
collective sanity, our sense of what to make of ourselves. Remove

the label, and one finds oneself—as Shaw remarked in the midst of
World War I—rejoicing at the killing of Beethoven because it was
Bill Sykes (the murderous Cockney of *Oliver Twist*) who fired the fatal
shot. Yet Shaw was convinced that the war once started had to be
won: therefore the label had to remain in place, and *Heartbreak House*
had to wait in the incubator for four bloodsoaked years because
"truth-telling is not compatible with the Defense of the Realm."

Are we at war in 2007? If so, with whom? Which subset of our
species must we choose *not to see* so that we may fight more single-
mindedly? Is it possible to conduct a war against a specific technique
of warfare (one to which most nations have resorted at one time
or another and to which some arguably owe their very existence as
nation-states)? What kind of truth-telling requires suspension during
a "war on terror"?

On some level, we probably understand that "war on terror" is,
as Gore Vidal remarked, "a metaphor, like War on Dandruff." The
actual foe has to be more localized: radical Islam, or the Crusader-
Zionist alliance, or radical populism, or the Great Satan, or
economic imperialism. Conceptual concoctions, ideals, motivational
abstractions. They are apparitions, yes, but plausible apparitions,
subsets that actually pay off: they deflect our sight from the objects
themselves, marshalling them into neat and tangible *categories*.

Yes, categories do pay off: always have. "Sir, I admit your general
rule" said Mr. Pope,

> *...that every poet is a fool.*
> *But you yourself may serve to show it,*
> *That every fool is not a poet.*

Which suggests several things, one being that the surest way to
demolish a label is to flaunt it. Another is that the label is not the
cause of the condition under attack: that is, foolishness is an attribute
of every poet, but it doesn't *make* him a poet—witness the case of
the attacker. I may be an infidel, or an acolyte, or a Tutsi, or a Mau
Mau, Cossack or Kazakh, Catholic, Communist, Rastafarian or
Republican, but none of those things are what *make* me a killer. For
that causality, you must seek elsewhere.

My murderousness is a private affair, a reserve I call upon when
sufficiently provoked, weighed against and in the light of cultural
values, of "me"-ness, religious admonitions, various forms of fellow-
feeling. *You*, however—yes, you on the opposite rim—you appear to
me simply as the *way you are*: the immutable definition, the category
minus the funny little frescoes.

Do we not miss those frescoes at our peril? My actions may be
horrendous or they may be bland. But if you take me for a *smudge*,
you fuel my rage. And, most certainly, you feed your own murderous
fear. Is this good for you? Or for me? Or the millions on millions
ripening on the collateral vine?

Poetry is of course many things, but it's *always* about seeing. The
poet's eye in a fine frenzy rolling, said Shakespeare. In that sense,
nothing sets this slim volume apart from poems of any time or focus.
Yet it may be helpful to the reader to know that many of these were
written during a *particular* time—that chimerical gulf between the
attack on the World Trade Center and the outbreak of open warfare
in Iraq. All are about very small things, whatever the size of the
canvas.

Their author? A longtime New Yorker transplanted to the hills of
western Massachusetts—messing with memory, sustained by love
and trying to track those damn frescoes.

Omar Shapli
Williamstown, Massachusetts

THEM

poems 1999–2002

by Omar Shapli

Short Storm

Thunder jars the linings of my teeth. The cat
has a comment. Protoplasmic memories raise
questions as the dirty little squall tucks in its
shirttails and takes off over the ridge.

THEM

They ask for nothing. Rain stings their cheeks
as their noses harden. They cultivate the knack
of intrusion and fiercely deny the possibility
that they may have been expected. Lakes lap
at their toes as their basted brains race past the
obvious contradictions: why the pilings (they
ask) why the groans and the tieclips and the
cornered racoons? Leave it open: let it freeze
and let it remain thus. There are consequences
to most things and the ruffled hummocks will
disgorge their guests when they're good and ready.

They hold their own. They look past the piers
and take in the evening. The acrid splatter
adds nothing but definition to the waters and
even horizons dig in their heels. Questions
grow hard as pedestals. There is mist.

They see it: they see and comprehend the
impending picklement. Grace locks their
ankles but some form of motion afflicts
them nonetheless. What wind advances
through my hair they ask, they who ask
for nothing. They are rooted, and wounded.
They stir their kneecaps and they adjust.

Love takes them, deals with them, sends
them to blazes. Frost tickles their nostrils.
They rattle their barrows and take in the
evening. Tricks are played on them:
wormwood! Wind is evident, is
everywhere, is not part of them. Lakes
break into diagrams. Starlight bristles.
Whole haystacks blow across their
eyeballs and sink in the simmering sludge.

They shrug off a shudder. Toe set hard to
sandstone they prepare to sing their silence.

Krakatoa: September 2001

but gandhi cried to rama as he fell

slice the
sun and

run

childe rowland
stumbles rubs
eyes
as krak
atoa
shivers a
planet of black doves

contours crack
through sac
raments and
here i

am
ai ram ai
ram

this

man this woman marking
flame then one an
other hand in
hand and
into
air
o
dare
exhale did
the welshman never

tell us love shall not be lost

antennae
tip away
as serried
voices
say their say in
all those tongues then
crackle straight for bedrock

killgod savors slaughter:
ground and grated flesh and bone

but deathgod has the
grander appetite the
very supplicant sinks
fingers selfward into
sternum uncouples
ribcage spills lung and
liver and whatever other
essence is still his
own into that
reeking gumbo and only
then does the monstrous
epicure allow himself the
benefit of a burp

killgod is deathgod in disguise

highhoned men defy deathgod: with a shout they
block his path and are consumed by him: wincing
now from indigestion he rolls on through the
collapsing canyons and claims his space

DUST

DUST

grace settles hard on the
crusted cicadas

terminus never had a chance:
towerghosts rain upon the
city like lost mayflies: the
thing that was there will
always have been there and
absence batters us like a club

Atta

He's learned to turn but not to land:
wasn't that always the lost traveller's
dream? To hold a single glinted moment,
then bank gracefully into chaos?

Geography of Slaughter

in proximity to the obscenity
note is taken of love admiration grief

further off
where real things weren't ripped
from the very notion of place
refuge is taken in dreams of revenge

Horsebreaker

Keep 'em out. That's number one.
Next is whoosh 'em away, send their
blackships scurrying everywhichway
to their flocks and walls and murderous
wives and failing that

failing that to kill 'em where they crouch.
Fill their crazy trench with its makers, cut
loose from life and yes from memory.

Circles back upon itself, does memory.
Blood, blood from the start. Cracked casings
litter the landscape. Had to be a time when some
god touched the cog and the dreary claptrap
lurched into lewd locomotion.

Things have got to be guarded, that's all: things
worth the daily descent into butchery. The woman
who allowed herself to be given to me: that's a
start. High assurance we've come to share,
web of friends in the early evening, thumpabout
son who *may* one day bring the blooded trophies
to a wife well guarded and proud: yes all that and
a general congruity, a way of breath.

Must a grown man's glory have to be to have to
know it's that verysame rightness feeds the beast
that longs to come crashing through the core? I
see it, yes: flicker of faroff campfires there on
our bedroom floor.

Don't like it: never did. Don't like the
rush of triumph as spear rips through
viscera to send some spry sweatgleaming

wannabee sprawled forever unstrung to the
earth that feeds us all: no, the tingle is itself
distasteful, like the sweetened emetic my
mother gave me when I swallowed the wiggly
spider. Triumph generates loss. Loss chills
to vengeance. Vengeance warms purpose
back toward triumph. Time's the deceiver here:
perturbates the process by splitting it in three.
I'm beyond that, now. Each moment blurs
prelude toward consequence. Comfort's
long scattered on the grass.

They're stirring early, down by the ships.
See? Beyond the crooked fig? Dust rising,
priests wailing: look at that. They want
us dead, that's all. Wives hauled off to
savage slavery, children skewered
midair or flung blinking from the
lip of these bedizened Skaian gates:
must be stopped! If we don't show
what *we* can do, then *they* will do it
tomorrow. Rip rein and have done.

Somewhere in that clattering cloud
the Runner sulks: he'll have his run.

History Again

It was never meant to be that:
never designed to slash at its own
dark beginnings. Hold hope for
smaller desires, scattered little
flashes that demand less. Pull
perception back a tad and play
with terror like a shuttlecock.
Mystery is permitted and fear alone
is not productive of size. Reconsider
the target: it may not be wise to
swipe off greatgrandfather's genitalia:
there are better cures. No never
believe hope cannot run backward:
Tamerlane may yet be held at bay
and Attila turn some other way.

Moloch's Altar (October)

One month later and
beneath the twisted
detritus the offering's
still being consumed.

Downed Tree on the Taconic

Up by the roots freshleafed and blatant across
both lanes. Two cars nuzzled against it in the
residual drizzle as a third pulls up as if to seek
another teat. Thunder crumps in the distance.
Men dismount and congregate. Two ladies
remain in black BMW contacting their veryown
satellite (they are complacent: help will not be
denied them). Guys spill out of the lengthening
lineup and speculate. Views are exchanged,
expertise alluded to. Branches are whittled at,
cellphones compared. There is jocular heaving and
tentative hauling. True evening looms as the two
ladies fidget: their genie is late. Joking falls off.
The great trunk clarifies, a guest settling in for the
night. Brows darken: annoyance pokes through
wornthin bonhomie. A last mad jab at the defiant
object most mercifully interrupted by flashing light
of towtruck followed fast by trooper squadrol,
both by merest chance. Trunk bedecked with heavy
chains now strains against itself qua catapult.
Trooper waves me into slingways and forth I hurtle
free as a breath and alone in the deepening dark.

Global Positioning

I am where I wish to be at this instant.

I am a good twelve blocks behind the place
where I wish to be at this instant.

The place where I wish to be skitters along ahead of me
like a helicopter's shadow: I am barely able to keep up.

Aimlessness strengthens in proximity to purpose.

Purpose acquires a purpose of its own in
close proximity to aimlessness.

I want to be where I am, but sitting down.

I want to be where you want to be.

I want to be anwhere else.

I want to be slower.

Of Tryntje

in pain and far distant
held at continent's length by
the immediacy of technology
she meets her loneliness alone

o god there must be something
more to it than that: some
irreducible duct through which
loneliness can spill, be shared,
find a common level between us

running yes among the mesas:
under loveland pass and sloping
down the high plains to the great
rivers: beneath the crabby snarl
of chicago traffic: breaking
surface through the droopy
nurseries of ashtabula oh yes a
feat of engineering to cause the
generations to remove their
hats as it stilts its way over the
hudson and into the midst of
so many flowers

well it hardly seems likely:
loneliness is a thing fed by
more vessels than one can know:
i reach out and i do touch something…
let it be her o god let it be so

No

academia revisited

piss upon the manner of
the sycophantic churl
ratchet his corruption of
the introverted girl

boil off the rivulets
that render him effete
trash the tacky tickertape
that complicates his feet

time has made it requisite
to calibrate the flow
clear the cluttered channels
and deracinate the hoe

wisdom cannot blossom
where the violet succumbs
and reason has it rough among
the cold chrysanthemums

John Dean Remembers His Moment

the mighty of this world
once beheld their
banners furled and
the brooks of high olympos
did run dry

and to my grave delight
though my guts
were seared with fright
they were none of them so bold as i

Weevils

What was it you said was going to hell?
California? The Post Office? Syntax?
If I do agree do I have to be interested?
If rank on rank of ragged parodies curve
wriggling on your retina like weevils in a
sieve is that a thing to deflect attention
from eurythmics? Or the rage of cats?
Or Beethoven? Be advised: military
architecture may breed its own necessity,
but where is it written that battlements
have got to block the view?

November 2001

Thin shafts of whitish
blue bide well beyond
the shadowed hills.
Carved solid, or seem
so: yet overhead a
wayward swampland
splashes east fulltilt.
Thirdfloor vines (still
madly green) dangle
and sway like unhitched
hawsers but trenchèd
brown impounds the
rest. Black cat wants
to come in. Pines
raise fulldecked
arms in some sort of
skewed exultation
made close to harsh by
screaming nudity
of all those others.
Thanksgiving's tomorrow.

War on Terror: November

Sigh and vie in slaughter of the bewildered.
Join hands: praise Moloch in the morning.

Dawn bleeds toward noon.

Summa Theologica

Sayyid al-Dawanni spendeth an afternoon with C-Span

So here's a broadbrained wellmeaning stack of a chap
who tells me my problem's that my religion never had a
Reformation. Overstocked already with gratitude for
that kind of outsight, I tilt my head and churn.

Reformation. Isn't that when a wildman rises against
general enjoyment of body and brain and tells us Only As
Is Here Written Shall Ye Henceforth Breathe Your Every
Breath? Thank you Sahib but we've had our Reformation,
over and over. Back near our millenium—eighteenth of
your centuries—that fellow Wahhab whoopsh'd his way
through the towns of Arabia like Calvin through Geneva,
with much the same result. Oh yes he booted the sensual
sheikhs and nice muzzy Sufis who thought the spirit of
God was in everything fresh and beautiful and ignited his
own bonfires of vanities wherever there were vanities to
burn. Some vanities are not abstractions: they have
toes and worries and occasional constipation. Still at it,
old Wahhab, three centuries down the camelpath and
fighting off the secular state arm-in-arm with Savonarola
and Knox and jolly Jerry Falwell. Yes they still preserve
us from satanic impurities: some thousand-plus years after
hot times in oldtown Baghdad didn't the mullahs block
the presses from grinding out a scholarized reprint of
our very own thousand-and-one-delights? If that's not
Reformation then Hus reads proof for Hustler.

Like you we've had our calamitous dilations: eyes and mind
subdued by chappies who clove to the bonethumping lie
that my Prophet meant functions of those pesky organs
to freeze at a given moment in time and memory. We've
had the others, too: the Khayyams and Khwarizmis and
wise old scribes who in your days of deepest darkness
transcribed and explicated that craggy bugger Aristotle

for us and for you. And when in your lands the ball finally
bounced from the boneyard was it Luther or Calvin or
stringy old Zwingli who knocked it for its loop? Not
hardly. 'Twas the ones who baffled both them and their
enemies: Breughel and Keppler and Geoffrey Chaucer—
Galileo, Cervantes and mad Will Shakespeare. The
fighters for perplexity against the frozen Known, the
ones who made their peace with the Deity and trusted
the tools He'd given them. And what about that sneezy
Dutchman Erasmus who sat up nights doing his best to
keep out the cold and dole out the word to old pal Luther
that that Reformation of his was headed straight for
disruptive bloodletting and severe blockage of the brain?
Humanism was what the cheesewheezing Rotterdammer
rolled across the table, and that, Sir, THAT and not any
number of theses fixed to anybody's rusty gate was the
enterprise that truly nipped our bottoms. Oh, we managed
to play in fits and starts but you, Sir, you rolled into it
smoothly as you did into genocidal horror and imperialism
and slaughter on a scale our maddest tyrants could only
cherish in their scintillescent nightmares. No not
religion I say nor putative Reformation thereof
gave you dominion over palm and pine, but
greed freed from spiritual inefficiency.

Love of God freed from the same dark hobble?
That, Sir, may well have been the Dutchman's
quest and that, dear Bwana, is a matter yet under
consideration in my house and in yours. Fertilize
your vanities, Sir, and we God willing may find
it possible to breathe a bit of life into ours.

Please to change the channel?

Humiliation

you obviously need this more than i do
sez the waiter as he tries to give me back
my stark five dollar tip: what went wrong
sez i bewildered as an englishman who has
just walked into a slammed door: there were
six of us six and wasn't the money flung with
grand panache upon this greasy table as all
departed one by one save one alone and
didn't i wriggle impaled upon the sharp
insulting gleam of his tightbuttoned cuffs

can't i ever get it right with money? all the
weary years when i couldn't face a taxform
the multiple seasons of scofflawry the fear of
opening any kind of letter that had the stink of
cash about it all these surge forward to form
the contours of one human face CAN'T YOU
LEAVE ME ALONE my daemon screams at
his daemon can't there be room for the corn to
grow and the buildings to crumble and the
birds to stay away from the cats?

sorry sez i a dumb mistake and the
superprofessional semblance of angry
reproach degrades to grit on the uneven
floorboards as he grasps at last that it's not
hardly at all the great waiterbaiter of lower
broadway nor even a peppertongued sketch
of a hayseed skinflint but just some poor
shmo who was last at his table and will
more than make up for the shortfall

Tillinghast in a Tizzy

AND WHEN
he asked as the
cellophane
wilted while
groceries
corrupted the
plastic sacks and
the hayseeds
fled back to
davenport
when and why and
whuffor?
taste
clings to the
edge of his
umbrella
while wholesale
turnabouts rework the
worst of the
latest tabulation
we are fed by
corruption
led by the
underbelly and
ruled by
thugs
umbrellas after
all are only
trash that is
shaped
in a certain
way but
taste's a
thing that
has to be trusted

McGinley Baffled

They are none of them ready just yet.
Confusion's a tide yet to recede. Digits
define acres of unpatterned bricabrac and
appetite hangs in the balance. Nothing to be
done said the dumb old mick but where
to lay the crooked forefinger when the
something implied by that nothing
rolls off the scale altogether?

They are not yet ready to do the thing
nobody recalls having asked for. Toenails
fray the insides of socks. Arteries thrash
against earlobes and fingernails draw blood
from palms in crazed determination to eradicate
nothing worse than the ghost of a yawn.

Well it took the old bogatyr Mourometz
hundreds of years to get up and walk and
then he turned to stone.

Stain

If time could begin with a bang then
whimper itself to extinction hard among the
pockmarked planetoids and vast dark cinders
that once were stars as they skid off and away
one from another till nothing's in sight of
anything (or wouldn't be if sight or light
had left any mechanism by which they
could be remembered), well then if time
could do that—start at one spot, then coast
to a halt coupled yet to the empty tender—why
grant it the dignity of immanence? Was this
dratsplatted coffeespill on pristine upholstery
ever a thing that was not going to happen?

Oh it takes time to do what there's
no time to do. Let the clock be a quirk of this
particular bubble of everything and hold us for
now in familial thrall, siblings to warthogs and
sandstorms and dying red giants, go what may.
Scrub stain, pay tithe—tomorrow's another day.

Bang

Before it: nothing? Jog your noddle.
 We were there, waiting to know what
light would be like. Heartbeat
echoed and yes was echoed. You
schematize a lockout singularity
when the pilot began to blaze?
A lie. Each incandescence emulates
the first, and every burntout lightbulb
owes its definition to the End of Days.

You certify our universe as a stack of coals
kicked apart to hasten its veryown demeez.
But then won't the silence that follows be
as finite a realm as this bumpabout minisecond
that separates it from initial ignition? Emptiness,
yes. A void as prickly as the balk before a sneeze.

By the Brook: Late Summer

Memory works hard, bends upon itself,
pushes where it ought to permit, seals channels
once formed by active commerce. Memory's
a weasel, is Loki the trickster tattling of matters
inconsequential as bureaucratic pomp or a
spleen swollen by desperate pretense.

Now here's something new: hole below my toe a
merest inch in diameter and barely more than
that to the inverse dome at its downside where
some solo vole set tooth to dirt and then
remembered. Or forgot: either might generate
abandonment. Was it the cat behind the flowers?
Or the crows who bring rotten branches crashing
from the big and doddering maple? Or did he
simply forget why he was there at all, a vole
sporting his volery? A bush taps my shoulder:
brook has its say.

Memory is not natural. What other function
discomfits indifferent to its own presence or
absence? Given half the chance it drills the
hundreds of tiny holes that let the past
into now, then when we come to rely on
that massive dilution of the immediate
it simply shuts down the spout.

Trim the bush: *that's* why I came out…

McGinley's Pocket Lexicon

Accessible: what you think might be graspable even by me.

Adventure is disaster modified.

Artist: a slogger for whom Task is an act of praise.

Beer is water that has lost its ambiguity.

Clothing: mousehole with mobility.

Critical judgement is ignorance with sword and buckler.

Cuisine: the high art of disguising necessity as whim.

Evil: anything deleterious to my economic interests.

Fanaticism is the enemy's heroism.

Flying: same old stuff with a dimension added.

Form in any form is praise.

God's grace: finding anything that had been lost.

Gunmen: enemy irregulars.

Laundry: systematic denial of time and transition.

Matter is energy down a notch.

Measured response: killing my enemy just a little.

Music's a farrago of frequencies which finally arrange themselves
into four clean functions: flattery, chatter, comfort, prophecy.

Peanut butter: antepubescent and postmeridian ambrosia.

Politics is courage hedged.

Professionalism: the ability to keep it moving with a minimum of talent.

Raw carrots are a shout in the ear.

Religion is a misstatement of the obvious.

Revisionism: replacing last year's lies with a fresher crop.

Road is a device for fabricating distance.

Shaving's a failure.

Song: a breath with ridges.

Starlight is a call to attention.

Tabasco is penance and reward.

Terrorist: an effective enemy.

Universality: imperial parochialism.

Walking is survival.

War's a concerted determination to not know what we're doing.

Window is having it both ways.

December 2, 2001: Special Delectables
for the Deathgod in the past 24 hours

Ten happy kids in Jerusalem.
Fifteen busriders in Haifa.
Seventy bewildered villagers a
tad below Kandahar.

Wedding party in Kashmir
kitted with kith and kin.
(See him wipe his flabby lips
and flash his stupid grin.)

Abu-X to the Mujaheddin at Fox News

suicide bombers are now to be termed homicide bombers

May God rescind at least *some* of your sins
for the favor of clamping that word HOMICIDE
to the doings toward which I now gird myself.
Killing's clearly the point of the act, the actual
loss of the bomber a cause of embarrassment in
light of that Koranic canon 'gainst self-slaughter.
Oh yes we've heard it said in numerous fatwas
that martyrdom willfully sought's no better than
cursèd suicide, a foul affront to the Giver of Life
in His exalted magnificence. Our weary riposte?
Suicide not being the prime intent, martyrdom's
honestly come by. They waggle their beards and
digest it not at all, citing by way of evidence that
very epithet our enemies flash to mock and chide.

You are kind to bruit it otherwise: o far less
misgiving to haunt my grieving family's pride.

An Ex-GI Tries His Hand at Translation

Mother Courage's Song (deference to Dessau and ol' Bertolt)

Hey Captain, can the humdrum drumming:
Let's get the troops out o' the sun!
Here's ol' Ma Courage, stocked and coming
With boots they'll need to fight or run.
Fucked up with lice and malnutrition,
They'll follow orders, win or lose.
So when you march 'em to perdition,
First fit 'em out with decent shoes!

> It's Spring again. So rise and shine.
> The dead have nothing left to fear,
> But if you're not one of them yet
> It's time to get your ass in gear!

Hey Captain, never let those doggies
Take time to wonder why or what;
Let ol' Ma Courage fix their worries
With booze for soul an' grub for gut!
A bowl of lice with fried gunpowder:
Hey Captain, that does not go well.
But when they're primed with my spiked chowder
They'll let you march 'em straight to Hell!

> It's Spring again. So rise and shine.
> The dead have nothing left to fear,
> But if you're not one of them yet
> It's time to get your ass in gear!

Clobbered

Take it hard and fast: why
stand frozen on the broken glass
waiting for the gulls to pack it in?
Burp twice and turn your back on the
crackling wave: head inland and up.
Landscape doesn't change but you
do. Things torn from your gizzard
festoon miles of malicious underbrush,
a trail made of nothing but you, each
step despoiling you of something.
No promise of replacement, no
inner rebirth: just a tad more
space for the lungs.

Take it hard and have done with it:
'sbeing stuck makes the morass.
Forget felicity: defer to breath.
Lift the tacky turdkickers and
swack at the yapping coyotes.

Busy Afternoon on Fulton Street

A sepulchral sigh and random drift to the left puts a
wellpacked bowlingpin of a man at the very point
about to be crossed by a charging dressedforsuccess
woman whose briefcase, barely able to keep up with her,
now smashes into her caboose as she into that of
said bowlingpin: oh a frozen moment of horror as
two dimensions until now mutually invisible are made
helplessly aware of contradictions

For a Wedding

Leana and Zach, November 1, 2001

Oh here's one TWO
that once was two ONES.
Wiggle THAT in your porridge
before the templates crack!
Boundaries fade but do not dissolve:
software sifts through the interlocking webwork but
something stubborn shelters the core.

Who bleached the crimson pajamas?
You call this *early*?
No its the *other* part I want you to explain.

Love godhelpus is the one thing that can't be qualified.
Its claims don't end at the county line.
It makes no bargains, cuts no corners.
Gets under the throwrug.
Messes up closets.
Violates gazebos.
Crops up even under the mulch.
And when you guessed
it was ready for a rest
didn't it pop out of desperate wishes and
deeply secret clutterboxes?

Love demands attention.
Requires submission.
Missing these things it
flutters off without the courtesy of a
thankyou note and settles down round the bend where the
pipefitter just said okay to the fuzzy wallpaper.

So here they are: two Ones, enraptured, terrified,
wobbling on the edge of a deep deep breath.
Just one more purely personal intake,

one's own private gasp, a struggle against the
force of ceremony toward defiant loneliness.
How damnably annoying to share that
perfect singularity, timed to the microsecond,
lung to lung, a single affirmation of the
separateness of things and somehow oh somehow
sense is made of the salmagundi.

> Engines race
> In place
> Clackataclump
> Clackataclump
>
> Give them grace
> Fullface
> And don't spare the yellow peppercorns
>
> Love is ready for them
> Courage too
> Prepare to taste
> The grand ragout

And savor too that other love:
the kind that comes from outside,
wishes and hopes like a splattery rain,
impertinent at worst, joyful at best,
a soaking of felicity to lose and regain:

its name is Celebration.

Shanty

max wasn't there
i didn't care.
bornagain regattamen
gave me a glare

torrible aghast
and drifting fast
they slipped beneath the shadow
of my mizzenmast

saul rose up
to the edge of his cup
suggested a colloquium
before we sup

i said NO
heel and toe
plopped his invitation in the
undertow

then came jack
warping back
splattering his spinnaker
to lose his tack

redwings race
from base to base
laughing at the laridae who
can't stand the pace

frogs relax
co-ax co-ax
i'll scrub the blubbertub and
wait for max

To a Computer

I began to wish for you a half century back: some
trick of suspending text in void unbounded,
rigging it with bulk, its own gravity, access
to the chisel at every point. My God it takes time
to get things right—shuffling about to see from
another angle, probing an infected limb to find the
hidden tick, the simple phrase beaming in abject
innocence while causing its neighbors to
gasp and groan and do their best to conceal
the pain. Weeks, months, years sometimes
to let the thing breathe as it must.

Paper's a bandage
and a prison: weight, before weight's called for.
This *sampo*, though: odd. In clumsy temporal
frame it fabricates timelessness. Not paradox but
physics, a thing beyond bars. I say it in a rhyme!
There can be no prison where there is no time.

A Teacher to Whom I Owe Much

Miss Hook is angry: roaring thumping
tearing at her clothes she
pounds her way
everwhichway
sighting somehow an
end to her hundredth year
and (one supposes) her life.

O gone is the quiet control the
Texan gravity the serene evaluative
interest thrumming outward to take the
measure of a man of seventy as easily as it
once did the desperate adolescent
he was and is.

Miss Hook fell down: they made her understand
freerein was a fractious laxity and set her hard
to bed. Miss Hook unsubdued did ring the
bedside bell and predictably dissatisfied with
speed of response she levered her proud form
past the restraining bar (highjumper fleeced
of pole) slammed face to floor and raged.

It's a rage that ripples backward year from year:
terrified kiddies clutch their desks.

Song

Perhaps it's true: perhaps grabberism
is indeed God's muscle, His right arm,
His tangible energy on earth. Haven't
the engines of the heathen shrivelled to
rust? The gospels of fellowship crumbled
to qualmishness and tongueclicking and the
changing of locks? You speak to me of
varied carols: I say I sense but traces,
substance longsunk in the spotted blotter.

Proof's in the bloody pudding: was our
species ever concatenated for generalized
selfhelp? We write, we speak our mind, we
play with wonderful gadgetry. It's a free breeze
fondles our foreheads but the water's not what
it was. Suggestions of a stench poke past
the ridges and thin veins of vapor crackle from
the jungle floor. Meadows blur: very hard to
make out the lowland from the heights. Yet I do
give you this: I begin to sniff the mote of a melody.

Voices in quest of cohesion. Rasps and rattles:
the terrible pain of nearness to song. Room,
room for the lungs! Things are squeezed, pushed.

Through the driveway gravel my toes detect
the tremors: tectonic migrations abirthing in
billions of tiny places: a pesky freckle in
Zambia, crooked toenail in Peru. And those
sullen battalions for whom Islam's a distant
myth: do they weep to see crackings of
casements that once seemed as far beyond
damaging thrust as the moon to a mosquito?
Oh not hardly. Exhaustion still anchors them

but they tug at the chain, a budge, whisp
of a drift toward purpose. They'll take to
religion if religion will brace them to the
task but they'll not stay with it long: it's
space draws them, space within and without
the ribcage, the vacuum that on its own creates
a thing akin to substance. *Power, is that how
you name it? Then I'll have some please,
have it if it kills me, as it will, knee to knee
with you in your hitek towers: a sweeping flame
to crack the limits of time. Are the two of us not
splinters under eternity's dirty thumbnail?*

*wang
dang
dillow dee
rattletattle dumpling
is my fee
four black stones
fifteen bones
half a gram of shimbleshamble
one two three*

Drought

a young journalist is murdered in pakistan

he's sought out his fellows and
they've fooled him
they open the gate to the secret place
from the very rim they beckon and they grin
we are as you are they say and
knowing this to be so he
sets his toes among theirs

their cheeks form ridges

they get to tie him up
they wiggle their pistols and
get to take his picture
they make him display the whole array:
the guardless gist that is them and is us

they cannot believe their fortune
they fashion the whisper of felicity
with a giggle and a shout they make
blood come out: they make him be dead

drought

drought

they race their tumbrils beyond the clouds
and deck their dreams with swirling shrouds

doorknobs hold their shapes
large insects tap their toes
tap
tap
tap

time's what it was

Saturday, October 6, 2001: Driving back to
Williamstown from Marlboro after hearing
the New England Bach Festival performance
of the *Magnificat* led by the epiphanic
nonagenarian Blanche Honneger Moyse

Whirlingdervish of an afternoon:
wind whipping up and dying fast:
clouds et exultavit marking,
reshaping bright blue continents:
huge spurts of sunlight sweep
those bubbling, oxidized hills
to stipple our windshield with
brief blurts of rain. Flesh and
bone still sizzle in lower
Manhattan. A thin and redhot
cloudwedge fecit potentiam
chisels away at Greylock and
damned if there isn't a rainbow.

Overheard by Tillinghast in a Boston Bar

(The Sevens: late Winter, 2001)

I didn't ask for it
then and I'll be
damned if I'll
ask for it now.
Pride is not so
dried up in me nor
song so lost in me that
mere fantasy and
confusion of spirit can
get me off this stool
and past the bricklaced
lions that separate
your street from
mine. I'll
dig my elbows into
wood and
face any
ratesetter who
cares to show his
weskut. If you
really think if you
really believe (if
belief is yet a
possibility
inside your
frozen pajamas)
that a holding of
public office will
grind my
doublehorned
calluses down to
ski-slope manageability and
render plausible the
blending of

horsepiss with
clothcertified
holywater then I
owe you the
profoundest of
apologies for
having been
good for the last round.

The St. Gaudens in Boston Common

For Ives it was Old Black Joe raising a rally
of ghosts who'd somehow lost the knack of
bending low.

Imagine the re-forming of retinas: consider the
shock to those who'd seen that war—seen or
sensed the very fact of slavery—to note now
before them that slogging line of frozen forms
each planting a boot to catch the weight of a
body tilted directly toward some fell purpose,
clear and shocking as Goya's chasseurs leaning
to the task of simple slaughter.

And there the young colonel, sternly equestrian,
not quite as larger than those others as a pharaoh
than his family, his fixèd chin projecting certainty
of imminent death as perhaps it truly did on that
day he led the parade (half cheered half jeered)
through these very streets and on to the mound of
corpses—their own—that would be its terminus.

The monument's Shaw's: that's clear enough.
These others are there to tell what it was he
died about, a prickly fit for passersby. Why
blazon the brahmin as paramount hero? Or
flip the palm at a damn dogooder? Oh brows
of every tincture shelter some fragment of sullen
chaos as they swivel toward personal purpose and
bend themselves back to the ways of Boston.

Lowell called it a bone in the city's throat.

Shake out the cooties and blink: it doesn't go
away. A fashionable formformer of some heart

once plucked from his recent yesterday an armed
formation he thought a match to his today and
quirkily enough the 54th Massachusetts tramps its
way still through everyone's discomfort and why the
hell not? Isn't its mission (yes SIR) exactly what it
was when fragile flesh and bone took pack on back
and made its way through and from a city
shocked at last to troubled silence?

Contrapunctus

He says he hopes to see his
mother on the other side, to
chat with friends, to
savor the taste of homefries
without the burden of grease.

Well maybe I say yes maybe these
good things are fragments of the
right kind of limitlessness, so
maybe they'll stay a bit when the old
gutbag fails and the scrimmages cease.

But me, I scorn to be a
prisoner of me forever:
may not my soul have better
things ahead than vanity
of selfdefinition? Must the
energy that shapes, is held
in place by my crooked finger
be still so crated eons ahead when
humanity's a mislaid ember,
effect bereft of cause?

No let me be then what I am now: a
dollop in a dingus that repels mere
comprehension. Let mystery be the
midwife and the fugue not pause.

McGinley Rips Up the Program Notes

Americans have the knack of taking warning
for flattery. Take that bolluxed bohunk
Dvořák and his grisly swath of a symphony.
Yes, yes, I see what it says here about darkies
on the riverbank deep in the melancholy
evening—yodelling redskins and Iowan
plains and prodigious energy of a brandnew
nation, gimme a break. What he threw us
was a fistful of grits with a rock inside.

Warning. Warning clear as nettles. Dark
forces from the start. You tell me serenity?
I say turpitude: grief deep and awful
prodding circumstance and forcing the
spirit to float free. Beat of native drum
and thrum of hungry depredator rattle hard
from the bowsprit: breakers upon us. Hear!
Black cry and red cry mingle repeatedly,
plainspoke, no subtlety: do you not see
what's acomin round the bend? Are you
not able to fear? All those voices once
submissive bake hard into what else but
stark calamity. Tidings of white sheets
and wounded knees finally filter to Spillville
and isn't it hardly more'n a decade since
Crazy Horse and his sad captains set
face to wind and raised a last brash
spear against all that grand new energy?

Back to Bohemia: the hops are almost ripe.

Noah

call the critturs fast:
recapitulate past ca
lamities but only en
passant don't
validate memory it ain't
corroborative it
squeecks like a knife
lobotomizes the present and
if allowed for just a single
fragile moment to slosh
through the scuppers it will
surely corrode the very
buttresses of ararat

January Afternoon

they're still here the
trees cracked and bent and
splintered like a
madman's secret furniture
nobody sweeps up: that's a
good thing: sweepup's the
last slat to improvement to
trim demolition

these woods are a song as fleeting as
any that rattles through my gullet: not so
much the pines it's the others
dark and low subtending snow or
crackling high to segment sky yes
thinnish undulant shafts
erupt in a fluster of
garbled twigs

joy's here doesn't need me to be what it is but love's
where I come in love's the eyes how else enfranchise
frail spires in sloping light below the
frittering firmament

men in windowless rooms ponder the stubborn tangle
afternoon moon can't quite recall its own lower
left quadrant: widening vapor trails set
boundaries to clouds and it's love
trundles me homeward

Beethoven's First Movement Cadenza to the Mozart D Minor

scrappy little rhinelander found that
the shore he'd hoped to invent had
already been reached which meant
two things: the shore had been there
all along and vanity's one pisspoor
compass

depressing news he said to cramer but when
offered the merest space by way of grace
didn't he fill it with an impenitent
hellothere peppered by pain
of a thankyou and yes
what less than a
highseraphic
rumpus

On the Old Stone Road, Alone, Late Winter 2002

(This was Stone Hill Road in Williamstown, unpaved, rutted,
flanked by thick woods, now rarely traveled. It was March.
There was fighting in Afghanistan. Enron had recently collapsed,
leaving its gleaming corporate tower to preside balefully over the
Texan range. In Massachusetts, mud season was setting in. It's a
speaking-poem: honor the beat and the breaks.)

walk
thump
taste of despair
pumping it
jumping it
thumping the desolate pump tada
to run
tada
to fear
tada
containing it draining the
westernmost fen and
tarrump it is bump it is
hardly collectable
barely corruptible
pumping the bottommost sump
tarrump
taking the dare
raking the air
to run
tada
to fear
tada
to peddle the pump to the west of the fen and

then

when

mysteries flush in the
profligate rush and the
nattering damned who can
turn but not land make the
sky
cry
the
jacobin nods at the
lesser gods and a
briarbush brushes my
eye
o my
a bush has set blood in my eye

(the trick is to waste
what the hangmen taste
as they wheedle the beast
to the nub of the feast
yes well before
the rattlesnakes roar
and the lampreys rise from the
chankly bore to
fasten their teeth in the sky)

the
trees
say
no
to the
retroflow
blinking it
shrinking it
making their moan
where slabs of stone
once rattled downhill to the
frozen gate and
don't we chuckle
to buckle the springs

as wondrous things
do rake the air
and take the dare to
wrap the sap in
farcical bark while
serious men
get cracking again with a
clink and a clank
in a texas bank
relining their paws
with a parachute clause
to float to earth from a
lofty berth as the
shimmering tower the
shell of their power
shivers to shavings and
bump
tada
tarrump
tada
time to reopen the dump

there
is
amazement in
the core of that shiver that
jiggles the liver when
gravel slips
through terraqueous lips
to send the feet going
awhishle awhashle it's

maybe

convenient

to grab at a branch to
spiral the dance as birds

tada
riposte
tada
with exquisite babble
reEvoking kabul
beware beware
the taste of despair
and where and when
do we find the men
to peddle the roadside pump
tada
and settle the festering fen

flames

still

lap at the chattering map
tadap
lakki coxsackie katanga and gurk
sap's arising
not surprising
grasping at grace in diminishing space
vetted to get it to work
tada
to run
tada
to fear
tada
to open the vent to a previous year
retaking the dare
raking the air
shaking out coffins ensnared in the hair and
bumping them
jumping them
over the chain to the
leftward lane
to hum

tada
to come
tada
consolidate fast
where the good things last
riddle and rattle and jump

to be where the bats
elude the cats
and rest on the crumbling stump

Seraph

Wings weighted down with eyes eyes eyes…
What else can it do but watch?

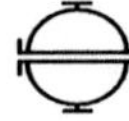

About the Author

An Egyptian-born, American-raised Korean War veteran, Omar
Shapli dropped out of the University of Chicago after falling in with
the theatre folk who eventually founded Second City (of which he
was a working member in the 1960s). He has written, directed,
and acted in numerous plays in Chicago and New York, creating
a principal role in Mac Wellman's *Crowbar* and, more recently,
appearing as Polonius in Richard Schechner's production of *Hamlet*.
While teaching his craft at NYU, CCNY, Williams, Emerson, and
Dartmouth, he has attempted to preserve his sanity by writing
poetry, some of which has appeared in *Exquisite Corpse*, *Café Review*,
Main Street Rag, *New Orleans Review*, and *Small Pond*, to name a few.
Omar's first book of poems, *The General Is Asked His Opinion and
other sad songs 2002–2005*, was published by twentythreebooks in
December 2006. He is married to the dancer-choreographer Tryntje
Shapli and has three sons.